LAUNCH

AND

LEAD

CROWN FINANCIAL STUDIES
IN YOUR CHURCH

FOCUSING ON THE BIBLICAL FINANCIAL STUDY

CROWN FINANCIAL MINISTRIES™

Crownuk.org

Acknowledgements

I am grateful to those who have helped me understand how to lead a Crown study group and those who have been students in our Crown groups.

Before Rhoda and I led our first Crown study we were able to learn from the Crown leaders in Gainesville, Atlanta, US. I would however like to acknowledge that the insights I have included in the manual owe much to the encouragement from time spent with Bill and Ruth Swain at The Apostles Church, Atlanta and Jennifer Helton who led a small group leader's training group which we attended in Chatanooga.

I wish to thank Mark Murray who has trained Crown leaders around the world over many years for his willingness to allow me to include the notes which he has crafted and form the basis of the notes included in *Launch and Lead* for the ten week *Biblical Financial Study* overview.

Contents

Welcome

Welcome to *Launch and Lead* Crown's financial studies in your Church. Thank you for your willingness to lead a Crown biblical study. You are embarking on a journey that will involve sharing with others what the Bible says about how we handle our money, wealth and possessions. This manual and DVD course will show you all that you need to know about how to set up your Crown small group. We will share how to do this the "Crown way" based on our experience and insights which we trust will prepare you to lead your small group members so that they derive as much benefit from the study as possible.

This manual accompanies the *Launch and Lead* DVD and expands what we share in this programme. The manual has also been organised so you can study those sections that you consider appropriate. The material complements the content in the *Small Group Leader Guide* and includes agenda plans and answers to questions. This manual and DVD is also for use by students if they are asked to lead a study.

We trust that you will be blessed as we share with you how to prepare yourself and your Church for this area of ministry. These studies have been conducted across five continents in almost one hundred countries and wherever they are used the results are the same. You will see people's minds opened and attitudes change as the study evolves and people warm to the core themes.

You may have previously led small groups and so we appreciate the time you will invest in studying these training programs. May God bless you as you embark on your journey with Crown.

Launch and Lead

This manual is intended to introduce Crown Financial Ministries' range of biblical studies to the Church. Pages 4 to 6 provide an overview of the study resources at the time of going to print. Please visit www.crownuk.org for all current publications. This manual provides detailed guidance on the introduction of the adult small group *Biblical Financial Study*.

This manual is accompanied by two DVD programs:

Launch and Lead – a two hour five part DVD including a sample of a Crown small group study class.

Introducing Crown to your Church – a two part DVD for church leaders and church members.

Every Blessing

Mark Lloydbottom

Mark Lloydbottom, FCA
Crown Director

1

About Crown Financial Ministries

Crown has offices in the five major continents of North and South America, Africa, Asia and Europe, where the ministry is headed up by Peter Briscoe who lives in Holland but hails from Newcastle.

Crown is an inter-denominational Christian ministry that was formed in 1976 and reaches out to all those who believe in Jesus Christ as Lord and Saviour. Our core values include recognition of God's ownership of all things, the need to pray about everything, and the desire to equip and serve others with excellence while teaching in ways relevant to different cultures and generations.

Crown's raison d'être

Over 30 years ago Howard Dayton studied the Bible to discover there were over 2,350 verses concerning how we handle our money, wealth and possessions. At the time Howard was running a property business. Following this time of study, Howard felt called by God to write a study on 'biblical financial studies.' The study that Howard wrote, accompanied by the book *Your Money Counts*, form the cornerstone of Crown's Small Group study programmes. Crown has available a range of books and study guides that are designed to provide understanding and practical tools to assist in the godly management of finances, wealth and possessions.

The UK leadership team

The UK ministry is headed up by Mark and Rhoda Lloydbottom. Mark is a chartered accountant who has enjoyed a 25-year career starting and managing three businesses. His first business was an accountancy practice in Bristol that employed over 50 staff and advised over 1,000 clients on all aspects of personal and business tax and financial planning. Mark built this business up over a period of 16 years and during this time also started a business known as Practice Track, which grew to become the UK's largest provider of solutions to accountancy practices for marketing to their clients and potential clients. Mark's last business was PracticeWEB; an internet business that today hosts and provides tax and financial content to more than 700 firms of accountants. So, if you're in business, the chances are that you have already read some of Mark's planning advice! Mark is author of *Clients 4Life*, published by the Institute of Chartered Accountants of Scotland, *Defining Edge Practice Management Strategies* and author of most of Crown's UK publications.

Mark and Rhoda were called by God to head up the work here in the UK in May 2006. From July 2007 to February 2008 they were based in Atlanta studying and working on the plans for Crown as well as anglicising some of the books from American English to the Queen's English. No mean task!

Mark became a Christian when he was a teenager and over the last thirty years has been extensively involved in Church life and Church finances. Mark was a co-founder leader of Bristol New Covenant Church (now Bristol Community Church).

Rhoda has been involved with Mark's business ventures since they married and has also taught in Children's Church for over 30 years. She was involved in overseeing the development of Crown's children's study guides. Rhoda is also a mother of three children and now has two granddaughters.

Within a year of starting Crown we are pleased to have leaders in England, Wales and Scotland. We know that God will continue to raise up those who feel similarly committed to this ministry. God has made clear that Crown in the UK is to fulfil His purposes to serve the Church and believers.

Crown's study resources

Crown UK has a range of study resources that are intended for use in the home and Church:

Church resources

Biblical Financial Study

This is our primary resource for adults to learn together what the Bible has to say about how we handle our money and possessions. The study covers nine essential areas that affect our attitude and handling of money, including such issues as debt, giving and saving. *Launch and Lead* and the accompanying four-part training DVD highlight everything you need to know about how to introduce and lead Crown in your Church.

Children and Teen Study-Stories

With children having no shortage of spending options it is essential to train them to handle money before they succumb to spending beyond their means and falling into debt.

Proverbs 22:6 instructs that a child should be trained *"in the way he should go, and when he is old* [e.g. and responsible for managing money] *he will not turn from it."*

By the time children leave university many will have accumulated debt which may not be repaid until they are in their 40s. The next verse in Proverbs (22:7) tells us that *"the borrower is slave to the lender."* Teaching children how to handle money is a number one priority. Make sure your children don't head down the same path trod by those who are in a debt-trap.

Give Save Spend – for those 7 and under

Give, Save, Spend introduces children to what the Bible has to say about how we handle our money. Children discover these truths as Alfie, Amy, Jack and Lebo try to save enough money to buy a puppy. As they find out how to earn, save, give and spend they also learn some important things about God. This book also has an accompanying parent/teacher guide with additional questions, activities, worksheets and a teaching plan for each lesson.

The Secret – for those 8 to 12

Follow the story of Nathan, Rosie, Luke and Bethany as they try to save enough money to go on a school trip to the Welsh mountains. Helping them along their journey, they will learn from David and Goliath, Elisha and the widow and her oil, King Solomon, Daniel, Nehemiah and Joseph. This book also has an accompanying parent/teacher guide which includes additional home or children's Church resources.

God's Way of Handling Money for Teens

A study for teens that will help them to enjoy life without becoming slaves to debt.

Business by the Book Small Group Study

Designed for business owners and managers the *Business by the Book* small group study teaches how the Bible can help you succeed in the business world. This six-week study contains solid scriptural teaching and thought-provoking case studies.

Resources for the home

Your Money Counts

A 166 page book that introduces a step-by-step approach to discovering biblical financial freedom.

Money Matters

This is a personal five-week study that includes five days of interactive Bible reading and two days of study reading. This study covers the same material that is included in the small group *Biblical Financial Study*.

Practical Application Workbook

This workbook will help you practically master your money. Use this workbook to develop a balanced spending budget, work your way out of debt and create a financial plan that works. This workbook can be used alongside the five week Money Matters study.

The Money Devotional

A 40-day devotional study covering spiritual and practical topics including: where is your treasure; tough times don't last; the poor; laws of prosperity; giving; materialism and many more topics that aren't covered in our other studies.

Children's Study-Stories

Give, Save, Spend, The Secret and *God's Way of Handling Money for Teens* are all designed so they can be used in the home.

The Money Bank

This savings bank has three compartments: Give, Save and Spend. Your children will learn how to budget and plan their finances. Start teaching children from an early age and they will learn the essence of balancing giving, saving and spending. The *Money Bank* is a Proverbs 22:6 resource that enables you *"to train your child in the way he* [or she] *should go."*

Business by the Book Study

Are you in business or a business manager? If so then this six-week DVD-study is an invaluable guide to learning what the Bible has to say about managing and growing a business. This study teaches businesspeople in all walks of life how to conduct business according to biblical principles. The six main topics include – having purpose in business; business planning; the importance of servant-based leadership; making good financial decisions; effectively managing employees and staff; the role of organisation and marketing. This study may also be used in a small group setting.

Insights into the world's financial economy

How does the world's economy work?

I recognise that this is not the place to discuss the many answers to this question. There have been many changes in the world's economy, none perhaps as great as the availability of unsecured credit, or what I sometimes call monopoly or 'phantom' money.

The growth of unsecured credit

In November 1949 Frank McNamara and Alfred Bloomingdale decided to go to lunch, as was their custom, at Major's Cabin Grill in the Empire State Building in New York City. On this occasion no one had any cash to pay for lunch, and perhaps somewhat embarrassed, Frank called his wife who came to the restaurant to settle the account. He determined that he would never again be as embarrassed as he was that day. Some months later in February 1950 he returned to Major's Cabin Grill which was one of 14 restaurants that had agreed to accept payment by a new card which Frank had called the *Diners Club*. In those early days purchases charged to the card were payable shortly after the end of the month with no interest charge. It did not take the banking system long to recognise that here was an income generating activity – give cards away and charge interest on unpaid balances. In the US the rest is history as unsecured lending increased every quarter from 1950 until the third quarter of 2008.

Unsecured credit in the UK

Here in the UK, the founders of the first credit card, The Bank of America, licensed their visa card to Barclays Bank who branded this *Barclaycard* when it was launched in 1966. Subsequent to the launch of this card others followed (e.g. Access which is a MasterCard brand) and these were subsequently followed by store cards. In less than 40 years unsecured lending spiralled and by 2004 total household debt had reached £1 trillion. However this household debt increased by more than 50 per cent in the following four years until in August 2008 household debt exceeded £1.5 trillion.

The deputy governor of the Bank of England reported in 2004 that he was happy with the levels of debt because they were matched by increasing property prices. However, unsecured debt was increasing and by 2008 unsecured household debt, where a household had any unsecured debt, was in excess of £23,000. One reason for this increase is that over the ten years to

2007 Government tax policy had changed away from companies owning cars to individual employees owning cars used for company purposes. As a result of increased tax charges on company cars many employees now own their own cars. In fact, the number of company-owned cars is reckoned to be less than 10,000 across the country. Another reason is the increase in student debt. In the four years to 2008 the economy was buoyed by an ever-increasing level of unsecured debt and increased levels of secured debt including remortgages on household property as well as increasing stock market values.

In 2008 and 2009 the global economy took a significant downturn and in the UK many issues had to be faced with UK banks receiving unprecedented levels of public financing, interest rates reduced; but none of these actions were sufficient to stave off the inevitable recession. The public's ire was raised when they realised how bankers, who had gone cap in hand to the Government, were with the other hand still claiming large bonuses. And politicians were cast as villains when details of their expenses were leaked to the national press. The level of greed at the heart of our economy was clear for all to see.

While these events occurred a little while ago they serve nevertheless as reminders of the unfairness that exists in society, while some point to the dishonesty those events revealed.

As a leader yourself you will have your own perspective and understanding of how the economy works, but one thing is certain: the events of 2007-2009 showed that the world's economy is very different from God's economy. The good news is that God's economy works every time and always will.

What debt really costs

In the Crown study module four we look at interest charges at varying rates. For example, if you were to save £1,000 a year for 40 years and *if* you were able to secure an average return of three per cent your additional interest would be £36,863. Contrast that with the gain the unsecured lending company makes at 18 per cent - which is in excess of £4 million! Compare that with a store card charging 25 per cent and their return is almost £80 million. No wonder stores want shoppers to use their own store cards.

So much to choose from

Compared to twenty years ago there is so much more to buy, so many goods that we need and an advertising industry that seeks to demonstrate how we should have whatever they have been commissioned to advertise. Marketing propositions vary but maybe the one that resonates with the majority is 'buy this, because you deserve it.' The use of cards and numbers has taken away some of the reality of dealing with cash and facilitated our ability to respond to those marketing propositions. So now we can pay for goods and not have to worry about paying the money back because it can be repaid in small amounts. And so the desires of the flesh can be easily satisfied.

The world's con tricks

It is not surprising that we spend money on goods that we decide we must have with money that we borrow. In so doing we accept the bait from the army of around a million people in the world of marketing whose job it is to make us want to spend. There are now so many commercial TV channels and some are devoted only to shopping. Online commerce is increasing – all facilitated by using cards and numbers as opposed to cash. Those employed in marketing accumulate information about our purchasing habits by analysing how we use our cards or which pages we visit on a website. Some of the marketing messages which they then use to encourage us to buy include:

- Buy now because you deserve it!

- The cost is only £x per month

- Amazing saving – *up to* 40% off

- Buy now; pay later…nothing to pay until 20xx

- Transfer your credit card and enjoy 0% interest

- Buy one and get one free (BOGOF was started by Iceland and is a marketing ploy used by many retailers)

- Four for the price of 3

- You have been selected…

- Cards make buying easier

- Savings of up to…

- Prices from…

Do you recognise some of those?

The intent is the same - to encourage you to spend. Someone once said to me that they could go on spending and keep saving money until they ended up bankrupt!

Saving

Levels of saving have reduced over the last twenty years. During that time savers have seen stock market crashes and interest rates at rock bottom – zero per cent in some cases. We have seen saving institutions deliver results that were much less than expected while some investment funds have been mis-managed. Those who expected a retirement income based on their final salary have found that their pension fund performance is now going to be based on money-purchase and so the return will vary according to investment decisions and prevailing market conditions at the time the retirement funds are required.

Giving levels have reduced

Most people do not give more than small amounts. While there are the highly promoted TV fundraising events and occasional disaster appeals, the reality is that most people give very little to charitable causes. Even in churches that teach their congregations to tithe often less than 25 per cent do so.

How does the world's economy compete with your faith?

I could answer that question on a much wider basis than this guide calls for! Goods and possessions compete with the lordship of Christ in our lives. Many have become conformed to the ways of this world as they allow their walk of faith and the lordship of Christ to take second or even third place in their lives. As debt levels increase we have to earn money to repay the debt or maybe we worry – which is the opposite of trusting. As we give less our lives separate us from acknowledging that everything belongs to Him and that we need, in part, to give in order to give back to God what is His.

Bible insights

The word Bible means 'collection of books.'

In the King James version there are:

- 66 books (39 in the Old Testament and 27 in the New Testament)

- 1,189 chapters

- 31,173 verses

- 773,692 words

The Bible was written over 1,500 years by 44 authors (their occupations included kings, peasants, philosophers, fishermen and scholars). The Bible was written:

- …in places as diverse as the wilderness, prison and palaces

- …on three continents (Asia, Africa and Europe)

- …in three languages (Hebrew, Aramaic and Greek)

It is a fact that many read the Bible to discover God's love and comfort, not financial instruction. If we wish to learn about money we may read the weekend press or buy a book on money management or even scour the web for articles and advice on how to increase income; people do not automatically reach for the Bible.

- Why does the Bible devote twice as many verses to money than to faith and prayer combined?

- Why does Jesus say more about money than heaven and hell?

- Why does 7.5% of the Bible refer to financial wisdom and instruction?

The answer is that God knows how money competes with the lordship of Christ in our lives and he desires that we learn and apply His ways. There is compelling evidence that our approach and attitude to our finances is indicative of our walk with the Lord and our true spiritual condition.

The Bible on money, wealth and possessions

More than many studies this one really does trespass in enemy territory. It invades the turf of a powerful adversary, attempting to cross a war zone laced with mines. The Crown *Biblical Financial Study* seeks to show how you can recover territory that rightly belongs to the true King. This study should be judged not in the light of what Crown says, but what the Bible says and what is revealed to you by the Holy Spirit. God's Word is grain, while ours is straw.

His Word is the fire that consumes and the hammer that breaks (Jeremiah 23: 28-29). The best way to align our heart and mind with God's Word is to systematically study what God has to say. Then as we allow God's Word to penetrate we should respond to His calling and obey. Do you recall that old chorus written by John Sammis in 1887:

> When *we walk* with the Lord
> In the *light of His Word*,
> What *a glory He sheds on our way*!
> While *we do His good will*,
> He abides with us still,
> And with all who will trust and obey.
>
> *Trust and obey, for there's no other way*
> To be happy with Jesus,
> But to trust and obey

NB: italics ours

We know Jesus as Saviour but as Christians we must submit to Him as Lord. The way in which we handle our finances provides a key litmus test to the extent of our submission to Him as Lord.

Do you remember the time when you were young, opened the drawing book and found the dot-to-dot page? As you join the dots you reveal an image you recognise. If you have young children or grandchildren that may be an activity you enjoy, or will enjoy sharing with them. After all you do not require eye coordination or keyboard skills to do a dot-to-dot!

I have discovered that it is only when you study the Bible and bring Scripture together that we see the picture of God's desire and His instruction to us regarding the way we handle our money, wealth and possessions.

We honour God as we make/earn money and in so doing we create the resource from which we are able to engage with the world's economic system. However, it is as we engage with the world's economy that we should follow God's economic principles and values, which as the Crown study reveals has its differences – hardly surprising given the fact that the world's economy does not exist to serve God and His purposes.

Objectives of the Crown study

The primary purposes of the study are to:

1. Encourage people to experience more intimate fellowship with Christ

2. Build close relationships among the participants

3. Help group members put their financial house in order

4. Challenge each person to invite Jesus Christ to be his or her Lord.

Impact! Ten outcomes (in no particular order)

While it is always easy to find and tell stories of people who work their way out of debt, it is a fact that Crown courses impact lives in far more ways. Here are a selection of the non-financial gains, outcomes, benefits and fruit from Crown studies:

1. You, the leader will benefit – this is an opportunity for you to lead and sharpen your leadership skills

2. Everyone gets the opportunity to facilitate

3. Those attending will start the habit of learning Bible verses – a habit that could continue beyond the study

4. The ten weeks offer an opportunity to make new relationships or deepen existing ones

5. Students develop a closer walk with the Lord

6. Some are challenged to *start* Bible study, others to spend more time in the Word

7. People learn to pray for one another and to share needs and answers to prayer: we were leading one group where three young couples all announced they wanted us to pray for babies!

8. Enjoy seeing group members build relationships - the socials are a great time to get to know one another better

9. The group leader meets individuals socially

10. If not born again, students can also be invited to accept Christ!

And that's before the benefits that students derive in better managing their money, wealth and possessions.

Crown's financial policy

- Crown Financial Ministries does not endorse, recommend or sell any financial investments. No one may use their affiliation with Crown to promote or influence the sale of any financial products or services.

- Crown's Biblical Financial Study, *Student Manual* does not give specific investment advice. No one may use his or her affiliation with Crown to give investment advice.

- This study is affordably priced because we do not want cost to be an obstacle to people who desire to participate. If you find the study valuable and want to help make it available to others, please make a gift to Crown: contact us or visit our website.

Four to eight week study groups

If you have elected to study this course with four to eight group meetings some of your study modules will be self-study. As the Crown leader you need to confirm the group plan and which modules are for self-study. For the self-study modules your group will need to continue the studies that you decide will be studied by the group; learning the memory verse, completing the personal study and the *Practical Application Workbook*.

Dealing with questions: at the beginning of each study meeting we recommend that group members recite the Scripture memory verses from the self-study modules. Check to ensure that members are also keeping up with the practical application assignments. One option, where the study is being conducted over four, six or eight weeks is to allow more than a week between study meetings. This is important as the practical assignments start with tracking expenditure for a month; one reason why the ten week study is recommended.

Another option maybe to add 15-30 minutes to each study meeting in order to allow extra time to deal with the additional feedback/questions from the self-study modules.

Group study

While you will see that we recommend the different programme combinations, the choice of group modules is yours. However, we strongly recommend that module two is included in every study as this has the essential DNA that lies at the heart of the *Biblical Financial Study*.

When you have decided which study modules are to be used you will need to communicate this with your group and have them complete their study table on page (v) of the *Student Manual*.

Please note you will only derive the full benefit from studying this course with a group over the full ten weeks.

No.	Module	Four weeks	Six weeks	Eight weeks	Your group
1	Getting started				
2	God's part/our part	*	*	*	
3	Work	*	*	*	
4	Debt	*	*	*	
5	Counsel				
6	Lifestyle		*	*	
7	Honesty			*	
8	Giving	*	*	*	
9	Investing		*	*	
10	Eternity			*	

* These are the recommended study modules. The weeks left blank represent the self-study modules.

Select and train new leaders

1. Set the stage
In the Crown Launch meeting, let your group know that, if they wish, they can train to be Crown group leaders. Whether they become leaders depends on their desire to lead the study and their faithfulness during the study.

2. Test the members
The most experienced leader(s) should lead weeks one and two. The co-leader(s) should lead weeks three and four. Then each member should be invited to lead one or two of the weeks. As a Crown group leader, you need to make sure that group members have access to the *Leader Guide* for the week they are leading. You may let them borrow your *Leader Guide* or, if you prefer, make a copy of individual weeks as necessary for the purpose.

3. Selection of leaders
You should consider only the members who are faithful during the study.

4. Approval of leaders by Church leadership
If the study is conducted within a Church, any potential leader should be approved by the Church leadership.

5. Invitation of leaders
After a person has been selected and approved as a leader, invite that person to lead the study. If he or she decides to become a leader, they need to be trained.

6. Training of leaders
For your small group members to qualify to lead the study, they should do the following.

- Study the *Leader Guide*

- Read this manual and view the *Launch and Lead* DVD

- Maybe attend a Crown small group leader training workshop – see Crownuk.org.

What's Crown's position on?
People often enquire about what Crown's position is on a particular subject. So, let's look at the structure the study follows:

What do you think or believe?
The study starts by asking students to look at some Bible verses – each week on average there are about 25 verses to look up. Following the studying of the verse(s), the students answer a question.

- Sometimes those questions are *closed* questions, where the answer is either 'yes' or 'no'.

- Sometimes a closed question is followed by an applicative question, e.g. why? Other questions are *applicative* only.

- Some of the questions are *comprehensive,* e.g. list the benefits for the giver that are found in each of the following passages.

- Some questions are *evaluative,* e.g. how do you think a person can develop the proper attitude to giving?

Therefore during the weekly study you discover what **you** think about each week's study topic.

Next, you meet with the group to discover how others feel and have responded to the study. For two hours you hear how everyone else has answered the study questions. In so doing you discover what **we** the group think.

Finally, when the study is over and you are about to begin the next week you are asked to read *Crown's* overview of what has previously been studied, followed by two, usually, applicative questions.

So, the answer I always give to this question is that Crown only seeks to direct you to what God has to say - it is His view, His instruction that we are interested in.

Taking a jump...

This small group leader training and the materials should be shared with your pastor/Church leader. They are the shepherds and we recommend that they are the first to be blessed by the study. There is an introductory Crown DVD that introduces Crown and its programmes as well as content on the Crown website.

This small group leader training does not discuss promoting this to the Church in detail – again, however we will briefly discuss some approaches to marketing.

Awareness tip: Once the Crown courses are part of your Church programme, you might wish to include a sign up sheet in reception for future courses.

Launching Crown in your Church

Marketing

We recommend that you hold a separate meeting to introduce Crown to the Church. We have include an introductory DVD and posters for display in the Church. In our experience there will always be great interest when the Church leaders are able themselves to give a testimony as to how effective and outstanding the Crown study is. A leader's recommendation is essential alongside other promotional activities.

Launch orientation meeting

A launch and orientation meeting should be held before the Crown class commences. The Crown leaders' section of our website includes a PowerPoint presentation and some notes that you may use or adapt as appropriate.

Please note that we discuss what needs to happen where you have a group of more than ten. In describing how to handle a large group (15 or more) situation, this allows you to decide what and how you wish to communicate. In other words what now follows is a full approach to launching Crown in your Church.

When to hold the launch meeting

Some churches hold these Crown launches after a Church meeting when everyone is together and child minding can be arranged. If the meeting is to be held after the Sunday morning service, decide if you will provide refreshments – something that is always appreciated. Hold this meeting *two to three weeks* before the first week's class.

Autumn courses

If you are running a class between September and December then, taking into account Christmas, it would be appropriate to have this class start before the **30 September**. Note you will need to order your materials from us at least ten working days before your launch meeting.

Spring/early summer courses

In order to ensure that all classes are completed before the summer holidays, we recommend that Crown classes are started **no later than 30 April**.

Ordering your materials

A couple will need the married couple's materials: two red *Biblical Financial Study* books and one copy of the *Practical Application Workbook* and *Your Money Counts*. A single person will need one of each.

	Couple	Single
Student Manual	2	1
Practical Workbook	1	1
Your Money Counts	1	1

You will also need a copy of the Small Group Leader's Guide (F103) for each group.

Please contact us for church orders and to obtain a church discount.

Length of this launch meeting

Depending on how long you set aside for any food/refreshments you should allow between 60 to 90 minutes for this launch meeting.

In advance of the launch meeting

Make sure that you have compiled a list of all those interested in attending and remind them to attend. They will need to know the cost of the materials and have either paid in advance or be ready to pay at the launch meeting. Leaders should read the Crown *Small Group Leader Guide* pages 4 to 14.

The launch meeting

Your introduction could include showing the student segment of the Crown DVD as well as any testimonies from those who have already been through the Crown study course. When you have shared your message with everyone we recommend you allow students to sign up for a group (maybe you could have group leaders stand by a table). You will decide in advance if there is likely to be more than one group, and in this case, if the groups will meet at different times in the week. We recommend that groups should not have less than six and never more than ten (including the leaders). Why ten? We find that this number of students provides the right balance in terms of group interactions and also allows everyone to contribute within the two-hour time period

The following are the key agenda points that need to be covered:

What is Crown, its vision, mission, people, global reach – this can all be found on the PowerPoint presentation in the Crown Leaders' section of crownuk.org.

1. Describe the ten-week course and its components: homework of about ten to fifteen minutes a day; scripture memory, practical workbook and praying daily for group members. Let everyone know the rules regarding participation – if you haven't done the homework you cannot participate in the discussion, but they will be able to pray and read the verses.

2. Agree the time and venue for the meeting(s). If more than one class is running the leaders will need to decide in advance when their class will run. When small group members are signing up they will then know the meeting time arrangements. You should also agree the ten weeks – do you need to pass on a particular week due to a bank holiday/Church event?

3. In order to graduate (and receive the completion certificate) as a Crown student eight of the ten weeks must be attended.

4. Child care arrangements – Church to assist if meetings at Church?

5. Let everyone know this is not a course where you divulge personal financial information.

6. Make sure students know that before the first week's study they know what their homework is:

   - Read *Your Money Counts*

   - Learn Luke 16:11

   - Complete the first week's homework (including starting the first month's spending tracker) and answer the four questions

   - Register on MyCrown at crownuk.org

   - Complete the *personal* prayer logs for the first week

   - Important: Make sure they only read as far as Day 6 – the Crown notes are to be studied in the following week. N.B. This approach applies each week.

7. In order to participate in the group discussions Crown asks that the homework is completed. At the beginning of each meeting students should be asked to confirm that they have completed the homework by holding up (briefly) their study manual – we suggest this be done upside down.

8. Scripture memory verse – please ask students to learn the verse as shown in the manual.

9. Let everyone know that the group *will* start on time, so please arrive five minutes before the meeting is due to start. The study lasts two hours and it is good practice to start and end on time.

10. Discuss the socials – there will be two for each group and these will be agreed with your Crown leader. Socials should be kept simple and not involve too much cost. An American supper approach can work with everyone bringing a contribution. They may be only for group members or include their family. We have worked this both ways – the larger the group, the greater the cost so this is for the leader to decide. The socials are really important as they allow friendships to develop outside of the Church or Crown meeting.

11. Everyone will have a chance to lead a study if they wish. This is a good opportunity to let future leaders know that their desire to lead the study depends on them faithfully doing the course.

12. No Crown class may be used to promote or sell any product or professional service. All discussions are confidential.

13. Ask if there are any questions and make sure everyone is happy with the instructions. Then have the small group members sign up for a group and go to meet their Crown leader – their first Crown meeting.

Meeting the Crown small group leader

This is the first Crown group meeting. At this meeting the Crown small group leader will probably need to make sure that everyone is clear on what they need to do:

1. Welcome everyone. You may wish to let everyone have time (a minute usually suffices) to introduce themselves.

2. Make sure that everyone has received their course materials (*Your Money Counts, Biblical Financial Studies* and *Practical Application Workbook*).

3. Make sure that everyone is clear regarding the week 1 homework – especially the need to start the first month's spending tracker at least seven days before the first Crown meeting.

4. Remind everyone that meetings will start and end on time.

5. Arrange the first of the two socials. These are an important aspect of the Crown study. These are times when you meet and get to know one another in a social and relaxed setting. At this first meeting we suggest you choose a time (Saturday or Sunday at 4pm is a popular time or lunch after Church) and ask everyone to update their diaries. If you try to find a consensus time you may find that the event doesn't happen because someone can't make it. You are the leader – this is a great time to exercise your leadership! We encourage you to find others in the group to take on the arrangements for the socials.

6. Have everyone complete the details of group members - you will find these in the back of the prayer logs (Pages 148-157). We usually pass this round and ask people to include name, email and phone numbers. We suggest you will find emailing everyone helpful. This might apply for confirmation of the arrangements for socials and, following the introductory meeting, you can send them confirmation of the time of the first meeting and an electronic version of the ten memory verses (on My Crown).

7. Let the group know you will contact them sometime during the course to meet up with them personally (and if you make this promise – make sure you keep it).

8. End in prayer. The recommended Crown approach is for the study to start and end with praying on knees - so let people know this and why not start right now!

Observations regarding the small group meeting venue

Where is the best place to hold these study groups?

Most churches will have established arrangements for small group meetings. Many prefer meeting in homes and I can see the advantage of this arrangement. We have some observations with regard to meeting in a home:

- You will need to make sure you have adequate seating for all students

- Students could be balancing their books on their laps if a large table is not available: Bible and *Student Manual* – remember that students should also bring their *Practical Application Workbook*

- We have found that the refreshment break takes a little longer in homes – taking the drink order, boiling the kettle and so on.

Some of these minor challenges fade into the background when the study is in progress. In case you're wondering about the observation with regard to the kettles – we use an urn in our Church so the water is hot when we break! While on the subject of refreshment we always seek to provide some on arrival in the form of a bottle of water. Others have the coffee and urn on the go at the outset.

Your personal preparation

With all the groundwork complete it is now your turn to be the leader. Remember that you should have appointed two co-leaders. You will be taking the first two weeks and then your co-leaders the following two. That means there are six weeks when other group members can lead. However, there is no requirement for anyone to lead and so be prepared to take up the reigns of leadership.

At this point we would like to discuss some of your leadership responsibilities.

With regard to planning and managing the study you are the leader and therefore retain responsibility. However, when you are leading a group your role is more akin to that of a *facilitator*. The dictionary describes a facilitator as: "a person responsible for leading or coordinating the work of a group, as one who leads a group discussion."

Thus, one of the keys to a successful Crown small group study is to minimise your contribution to the group discussions in order that you can focus on keeping the study progressing. Encourage participation and make sure that everyone participates each week. Praying for your group members is also very important. Group members will see how God answers prayer during the ten weeks and this is a key for some students in encouraging and developing their prayer life.

You may have done the study before (or more likely you will do so in the future). We recommend that you redo the study on each occasion. It is very tempting (saves time) to dust off the *Student Manual* and rely on your past notes. We encourage you to redo the study each time you lead. You will find God speaking to you each time you complete the study – and your fresh prayer logs will also be waiting for completion at the back of the book!

Your first Crown study has arrived

The *Small Group Leader Guide* includes an agenda with suggested timings and space for you to record your own timetable. Wherever possible, adhere to these. Within the two hours you may wish to allocate time for a refreshment break – after day three of the study often seems to work well. You may need some flexibility when moving from one day's question to another, but you will find that the timings represent a good time allocation for the two hour study.

You will also see that the *Small Group Leader Guide* has some suggested answers – these are usually brief. After being a Crown leader for the first two lessons, I stopped looking at the Crown answers as I wanted to respond to the questions as I felt led and as I understood the answers and how the study applied to me. In fact, the first study Rhoda and I led was with our own Church leaders – many of whom were trained Bible scholars and I found their insights and understanding very helpful. In the same way, be prepared to learn from your students – and record any insights that you find interesting. In this way your students help you develop as a leader.

1. Starting on time
I usually do just that, start on time – to the minute. I find if you wait, you will still not have everyone present and more significantly, you will be communicating to everyone that it's okay to be late. You respect everyone's time when you start on time.

2. Opening in prayer
Either ask one or two people to pray or allow a time of open prayer, or ask everyone to pray a short prayer around the group.

Crown asks that everyone prays on their knees. We believe that this is an act of reverence to our Father and is a demonstration of our submission to Him. As we come into the presence of the most Holy God, let us do so by bending our knees to Him. We live in times when our country needs to turn to Christ, let us individually bow our knee and go low before God.

3. Memory verse
If you are leading you can start with yourself or the person next to you and then move around the room reciting the verse and scripture reference.

When someone joins the class late we suggest you have them recite the verse *just before* it is their turn to read one of the Bible verses.

If someone misses a class then the next week, when it comes to their turn they will need to recite the verse they missed. That way, you will ensure that everyone learns *all* ten verses.

4. Homework completed?
Have the group briefly hold their *Student Manual* and *Practical Application Workbook* up to show they have done their week's work. This is part of the accountability process.

Forward to the six days studies
We will cover both modules one and two as the first module is not representative of the subsequent studies.

5. Module one

This is your first week, so allow time to welcome everyone and thank them for coming. You may wish to remind them that they will not be required to share anything that is financially personal to them. It is helpful to adhere to the Crown guidelines in order to avoid straying into counselling or dealing with individual group member's financial problems.

Starting with any group member you care to choose, ask them to share what they learned from reading *Your Money Counts*. Depending on the number in your group and taking into account how well they know one another, maybe you could also ask them to share something about themselves, their family, their testimony. Let each person have a time allocation (this may well be between seven and ten minutes) - this is a good place to start group time management.

Tip: Write the Bible page number for each verse in your *Student Manual* – other group members may wish to do this as well as this can be a good time saver, and can be helpful for those who can't easily locate a particular verse.

There are then three Bible verses which again you can ask each student to comment on. This will not be the format for the following nine weeks, but it will serve as an opportune occasion to allow the group to listen to one another. Look out for any group member that remains silent – encourage them to participate, while also gracefully reigning in any member that allocates more time to their viewpoint than you consider appropriate.

Tip: Encourage your students to start learning next week's verse at the beginning of the week – it is the longest verse they will have to learn – and, possibly the most significant one – often it is this verse that people recall a long time after the course has finished.

---

6. Review of next week

Each week there is a 10-minute time slot to discuss what needs to be done during the following week. This provides an opportunity to review what needs to be done in the *Practical Application Workbook*. *Launch and Lead* has some notes on the *Practical Application Workbook* that you may find helpful to review. However, reading the *Practical Application Workbook* notes is the best introduction to sharing what needs to be done over the coming week.

7. Prayer logs

Each week collect prayer requests. Encourage everyone to share personal/family requests, rather than friends, contacts. Let everyone know that during the study they should pray daily for all members.

8. End in prayer

Pray with the group on their knees.

Module two

Before we look at the next stage of the study, let us look in further detail at the format for the second study. This is entitled "God's part and our part", and is, for some, the most significant study because it is in this week's memory verse and study that we learn that everything belongs to God. Students may be a little apprehensive of completing the Deed of Ownership and having this witnessed, but again let everyone know that if they are witnessing, they should not look at what has been written. As you will see in the workbook, this is <u>not</u> a legal document.

Students will also be continuing to record their income and expenditure which they will do for the next three weeks in order to build up a one month pattern of their expenditure. They will require this information to assist them with later weeks when they look at budgeting.

Students will also have completed their personal financial statement.

Allocate some time to reviewing what the homework was and making sure you answer any questions that arise. This will settle in students' minds the importance of the homework as an integral aspect of the curriculum.

Studying the day's homework

There are 21 verses/passages of scripture this week, so now is a good time to hone your facilitation skills. Day two comprises three passages and two questions. We recommend that you ask the next three students (in succession) to read the verses from Deuteronomy, Psalm 24 and 1 Corinthians and then go back to the first person for the answers, followed by the second and third student. Depending on how you feel about the responses, you have the option to ask others to share their response: "does anyone else have anything to add?"

That pretty much covers the approach to the individual days!

Good facilitation of this part of the Crown group includes:

• Not allowing students to share at too intimate a level, especially where the leader perceives that counsel is required.

- Not allowing any 'financial experts' to start giving advice.

Tip: If you sense that the class is moving in a way that makes you uncomfortable, you could say something like: "We're moving away from the study into counselling...we need to get back on track" or "we need to follow this up outside of the class."

Encourage; give positive feedback, "thank you, that's a good point".

- If you need to move on...just move on, "right now let's move onto day three..."

This format is tried, tested and it works

Crown studies have been taught in almost 100 countries and to over 80 million people. We have an approach that works and we encourage you to follow this format as closely as possible. Part of your role as leader is to develop other leaders and in the first two weeks you have the opportunity to lead the way and show how it's done. You may also be training your two co-leaders and then other group members will have the opportunity to follow your example. They need to know that they should follow the format. If you ask anyone else to facilitate the group you should spend some time with them going through how to run the next class.

Socials

Some groups arrange the food so that everyone brings along something to eat including:

- crisps/drinks

- dips

- salad

- main course

- dessert

and so on.

This then avoids one person being responsible for all the catering and also reduces costs. Having said that, it is for the group to decide what they wish to do – that could include an outing, bowling, picnic and so on.

Graduation

Provided students have completed eight or more of the lessons, they graduate. We will send you a PDF certificate which you can print out, sign and hand out. Would your Church leader hand out the certificates in Church? This is an opportunity for the Crown class to be highlighted in the Church and maybe one or two could give a testimony.

Time with your students

You should seek to meet socially outside of the small group with each of the students. This could be for coffee or lunch. Use this time to find out how they feel about the course as well as getting to know them better on a one on one or couple by couple basis. (Avoid single meetings with opposite sex).

Follow up to your Crown study

- Are there others in your Church that would be interested in the next Crown study?

- Would the business owners and/or managers like to go through the Business by the Book six week study?

- Would you like to use the Crown children's study guides in your Children's Church?

- Would you like to become a Crown volunteer? If so, please contact us.

Everyone at Crown trusts that you will be blessed as you go through your Crown study.

Please contact us or visit our website at www.crownuk.org.

An overview of the 10 study modules

The *Biblical Financial Study* comprises approximately 20-25 verses each week while there is a further raft of verses in each week's study notes. You may wish to refer to these while you read these introductory notes as well as focusing on a general overview of the content and on each week's module.

Module one
Getting started

The first week allows the group to become acquainted with one another. Each student should have read *Your Money Counts* and will be asked to share some of the key points they have learned from this book. Each student has approximately 6-10 minutes to speak - your agenda on Page 10 of the *Small Group Leader Guide* has some suggested questions. If you wish to employ other 'warm up and share' questions please do. The objectives for the first week are to encourage students to participate, to get to know one another and to experience the group dynamics of everyone participating rather than having someone lead/teach.

By the end of this week you should have everyone aware of what to do for homework:

- Complete the personal study in the red *Student Manual*

- Complete the practical homework on the *Practical Application Workbook*

- Learn the memory verse

- Complete the prayer log

Students should also be getting used to the recommended approach of praying on their knees.

You should also have an agreed date and venue for the first group social.

This week we look at spiritual and practical reasons why the Bible contains so much regarding how we handle money and possessions. How we handle our money has a significant impact on the intimacy of our relationship with Christ. We learn that a more intimate relationship with Christ is the 'true riches' in life. Money is a primary competitor with Christ for the lordship of our lives.

Practically, the Lord knows we need wisdom in using money. He shows in Scripture His principles for working, earning, spending, saving, investing, giving, getting out of debt and teaching children how to handle money. If people have been taught anything about God's way of handling money, it has usually been about giving while the principles of earning and spending have rarely been taught. Therefore, God's people have not always realised how to manage all their money from God's perspective.

At the end of this study remember to encourage students to start learning next week's memory verse. It is the longest and in many respects the most powerful and impactful.

Module two
God's part and our part

God is the owner of everything – the earth, silver, gold, land, animals, you and me. Everything. God is in ultimate control of every event. God will provide for our needs.

God is both predictable and unpredictable. He is predictable in His faithfulness to provide. He is unpredictable in how He will provide. In the Bible, the Lord provided for His people in many different and often unexpected ways. The same Lord who fed manna to the children of Israel during their forty years of wandering in the wilderness, and who fed 5,000 with only five loaves and two fish, has promised to provide our needs. This is the same Lord who instructed the ravens to feed Elijah with bread in the morning and bread and meat in the evening.

Our responsibilities with money

We are stewards of God's possessions - a steward is a manager of someone else's possessions. As stewards we are called to be faithful with all that we have. Not only are we to be faithful stewards of the ten per cent that we give but also of the other ninety per cent. All that we have is the Lord's and we are to manage it in a way that is pleasing to Him.

We are to be faithful in little things

If we are faithful with small things, God can trust us with greater responsibilities. We must not spend our money in ways that we know would displease Him because this would make us unfaithful stewards.

Our responsibility with money

When we are faithful we will benefit in three ways:

1. We will grow closer to Jesus Christ

Faithfully applying God's financial principles will help you grow in your love for Christ.

2. We will develop godly character

God uses money to reveal our character. How we handle money is an external indicator of our true spiritual condition. You can tell a lot about the character of people by examining how they handle money. For example, are they dishonest or honest? Do they gamble/game or do they give?

3. We will begin to have financial stability

As we apply God's principles to our finances, we will begin to spend more wisely, start saving for the future, and give more to the work of Christ.

Module three
Work

God created work for our benefit

God placed Adam in the Garden of Eden to work and take care of it. Thus the Lord created work for our benefit in the sinless environment of the Garden of Eden.

God's perspective of work

Work is necessary for the Bible tells us that we should work for six days, and if someone does not work, they should not eat.

- Work develops our character

- We work for Christ

God's work responsibilities:

A. God gives us our job skills

Because God has given each person unique skills and talents, Scripture does not elevate any honest occupation above another. A wide variety of jobs are represented in the Bible. David was a shepherd and a king. Luke was a doctor. Lydia was a retailer who sold purple fabric. Daniel was a Government worker. Paul was a tentmaker. And finally, the Lord Jesus was a carpenter.

B. God gives us our success
Joseph is an example of God helping a person to succeed. We have job responsibilities, but we need to recognise that it is ultimately God who gives us success.

C. God gives promotion and advancement
As much as it may surprise you, people do not totally control whether they will be promoted. The Lord ultimately controls success and promotions.

Our work responsibilities:

A. We are to work hard
"Whatever your hand finds to do, do it with all your might" (Ecclesiastes 9:10). *"… the diligent man prizes his possessions"* (Proverbs 12:27). Scripture, while condemning laziness, encourages diligence and hard work. *"One who is slack in his work is brother to one who destroys"* (Proverbs 18:9). Paul's life was an example of hard work *"…we worked night and day, labouring and toiling so that we would not be a burden to any of you…. In order to make ourselves a model for you to follow"* (2 Thessalonians 3:8-9).

B. We are not to overwork
Hard work, however, should be balanced by the other priorities of life. If your job demands so much of your time and energy that you neglect your relationship with Christ or your loved ones, then you are working too hard. Exodus 34:21 reads, *"Six days you shall work, but on the seventh day you shall rest; in ploughing time and in harvest you shall rest"* (NKJV). Rest can become an issue of faith. Is the Lord able to make our six days of work more productive than seven days? Yes! The Lord instituted weekly rest for our physical, mental, and spiritual health.

C. We are to be honest
"Do not steal. Do not lie. Do not deceive one another" (Leviticus 19:11).

D. We are to honour our employers
Godly people always honour their superiors. 1 Peter 2:18 reads, *"Slaves,* [employees] *submit yourselves to your masters* [employers] *with all respect, not only to those who are good and considerate, but also to those who are harsh."*

E. We are to honour fellow employees and never slander them

"Do not slander a servant [employee] *to his master* [employer], *or he will curse you, and you will pay for it"* (Proverbs 30:10).

Module four
Debt

The Bible does not say that using debt is sin, but it does discourage it. Debt is money or possessions which one person is obligated to pay to another. Debt includes money owed to banks, friends, relatives, credit card companies and finance companies.

1. What Scripture says about debt:

A. Debt is discouraged

"Let no debt remain outstanding..." (Romans 13:8).

B. Debt is considered slavery

"The rich rule over the poor, and the borrower is servant to the lender" (Proverbs 22:7). We do not have full freedom to decide where to spend our income if we are obliged to repay debt.

C. In the Old Testament:

1. Debt was a curse for disobedience

"If you do not obey the Lord your God...all these curses will come upon you... The alien who lives among you will rise above you higher and higher.... He will lend to you, but you will not lend to him..." (Deuteronomy 28:15, 43-44).

2. Freedom from debt was a reward for obedience

"If you fully obey the Lord your God...all these blessings will come upon you.... You will lend to many nations but will borrow from none" (Deuteronomy 28:1-2, 12).

D. Debt presumes on the future

When we get into debt, we assume that we will earn enough income in the future to pay the debt. The Bible discourages presumption. *"You who say, 'Today or tomorrow, we will go to this or that city, spend a year there, carry on business and make money.' Why, you do not even know what will happen tomorrow.... Instead, you ought to* say, 'If it is the Lord's will, we will live and also do this or that'" (James 4:13-15).

E. Repay what is borrowed

"The wicked borrow and do not repay, but the righteous give generously" (Psalm 37:21). God's people should pay their debts as promptly as they can. *"Do not withhold good from those who deserve it, when it is in your power to act. Do not say to your neighbour, 'Come back later; I'll give it tomorrow' - when you now have it with you"* (Proverbs 3:27-28).

Some factors that lead to debt

- Lack of knowledge: Most people have not been trained to handle money God's way.

- Lack of planning and discipline: Many people spend impulsively because they have no written plan or budget to ensure that spending does not exceed income.

- Indulgence: Some people spend in an attempt to satisfy fleshly desires.

- Circumstances: Sometimes people use debt when they experience unexpected emergencies, such as an illness or loss of a job.

2. How to get out of debt

Here are seven steps for getting out of debt:

1. Pray

In 2 Kings 4:1-7 a widow was threatened with losing her children to her creditor, and she asked Elisha for help. Elisha told her to borrow empty jars from her neighbours. The Lord multiplied her only possession, a little oil, and all the jars were filled. She sold the oil to pay her debts and free her children. The same God who provided for the widow is interested in helping us becoming free from debt. The most important step is to pray and seek the Lord's help and guidance.

2. Accumulate no new debt

3. List all your debts and everything you own

List your debts to determine your current financial situation. Then decide whether you should sell any possessions to reduce debt.

4. Use a written spending plan or budget

Develop a written spending plan to ensure that spending does not exceed income.

5. Establish a repayment plan for each debt

Most creditors are willing to work with people who honestly want to repay their debt, communicate regularly and follow through with their commitment. Try to pay off the smallest debts or those with the highest interest rate first. Once you have paid off the first debt, add that payment amount to the regular payment for the second one that you want to pay off. Then, when that one is paid off, apply both payments to the next debt and so forth until all debts are repaid.

6. Consider earning additional income

Many people hold jobs that simply do not produce enough income to meet their needs even if they spend wisely. They may need to earn additional income to get out of debt.

7. Reduce spending

Some people need to lower their spending to get out of debt.

When is debt acceptable?

Scripture is silent on when debt is acceptable. In our opinion, it is permissible to owe money for your business, to buy a home using a mortgage, or education for your trade or vocation. If you borrow for any of these uses, follow these guidelines:

- Make debt the exception and not the rule

- Plan to repay what was borrowed as soon as possible

- Create a written repayment plan.

3. Cosigning or guaranteeing

Cosigning or guaranteeing relates to debt. Anytime you cosign, you become legally responsible for the debt of another. It is just as if you borrowed the money and gave it to the friend or relative who is asking you to cosign/guarantee the loan. The Bible discourages cosigning. Proverbs 17:18 reads, *"It is poor judgment to cosign another's note, to become responsible for his debts."* However, a university may require a guarantee for the halls of residence fees and, in our opinion that is a necessary guarantee and is an extension of parental responsibilities.

Module five
Counsel

God encourages us to seek counsel before making important financial decisions. *"Listen to advice and accept instruction, and in the end you will be wise"* (Proverbs 19:20). *"The way of a fool seems right to him, but a wise man listens to advice"* (Proverbs 12:15). Some people avoid seeking counsel from others because of their pride. They view asking for advice as a sign of weakness, but this is contrary to what the Bible teaches. We should seek counsel to secure insights, suggestions and alternatives that will help us make the best decisions. Scripture encourages us to obtain advice from several sources.

1. Spouse

If you are married, the first person you need to consult is your spouse. The husband and wife are one, and they need each other to make proper decisions. Women tend to be gifted with an accurate intuitive nature. Men tend to focus more on the facts.

2. Parents

Another source of counsel is our parents. *"My son, keep your father's commands and do not forsake your mother's teaching. Bind them upon your heart forever; fasten them around your neck. When you walk, they will guide you; when you sleep, they will watch over you; when you awake, they will speak to you"* (Proverbs 6:20-22). Our parents have the benefit of years of experience and they know us well.

3. Godly people

We should also ask advice of godly people who know how to apply the principles found in the Word of God. Experienced people who know the Bible are especially valuable counsellors. The Bible makes this remarkable claim about itself: *"For the word of God is living and active. Sharper than any double-edged sword...it judges the thoughts and attitudes of the heart"* (Hebrews 4:12). The Bible is a living book that our Lord uses to communicate His direction to all generations. Its truths are timeless. Psalm 119:98-100 reads, *"Your commands make me wiser than my enemies.... I have more insight than all my teachers, for I meditate on your statutes. I have more understanding than the elders, for I obey your precepts."*

4. Many counsellors

Each of us has a limited range of knowledge and experience; we need the input of others to give us insight and stimulate our thinking with alternatives we would not otherwise consider. *"Plans fail for lack of counsel, but with many advisers they succeed"* (Proverbs 15:22). *"For lack of guidance a nation falls, but many advisers make victory sure"* (Proverbs 11:14).

However we are expressly instructed to avoid fortune-tellers, mediums and spiritualists

The Bible tells us never to seek the advice of fortune-tellers, mediums or spiritualists: *"Do not turn to mediums or seek out spiritists; for you will be defiled by them. I am the Lord your God"* (Leviticus 19:31). Read this next passage carefully: *"Saul died because he was unfaithful to the Lord; he did not keep the word of the Lord and even consulted a medium for guidance, and did not inquire of the Lord..."* (1 Chronicles 10:13-14). Saul died, in part, because he went to a medium. We should avoid any methods they use in attempting to forecast the future, such as horoscopes and all other occult practices.

Module six
Lifestyle

1. Learn to be content

The apostle Paul wrote in 1 Timothy 6:8: *"if we have food and clothing, we will be content with that."* If this were an advertisement it would read something like this, "If you can afford the finest food, wear the latest fashions, and live in a beautiful home, then you will be happy." Our society operates on the assumption that more is always better and that happiness is based on acquiring things.

Paul writes in Philippians 4:11-13: *"I have learned to be content whatever the circumstances. I know what it is to be in need, and I know what it is to have plenty. I have learned the secret of being content in any and every situation, whether well fed or hungry, whether living in plenty or in want. I can do everything through Him who gives me strength."*

Paul learned to be content. We are not born content; rather, we learn contentment.

2. Learn to avoid coveting

Coveting means to crave another's property, and it is prohibited throughout Scripture. The last of the Ten Commandments is, *"You shall not covet your neighbour's house. You shall not covet your neighbour's wife or his male servant or his female servant or his ox or his donkey or anything that belongs to your neighbour"* (Exodus 20:17).

Greed is similar to coveting: *"But among you there must not be even a hint of sexual immorality, or of any kind of impurity…. For of this you can be sure: No immoral, impure or greedy person - such a man is an idolater - has any inheritance in the kingdom of Christ and of God"* (Ephesians 5:3, 5).

3. Do not determine your lifestyle by comparing it to others

Some use comparison to justify spending more than they should. Many have suffered financially because they tried but could not afford to "keep up with the Joneses." Someone once said, "You can never keep up with the Joneses. Just about the time you've caught up with them, they go deeper into debt to buy more things!"

4. Freely enjoy whatever you spend in the 'Spirit'

Prayerfully submit spending decisions to the Lord. Seeking the Lord's direction does not mean that we will never spend for anything other than a basic necessity.

5. Make every effort to live more simply

Every possession requires time, and often money, to maintain. Too many or the wrong type of possessions can demand so much time or money that they harm our relationships with the Lord and others. A quiet, simple life is the safest environment for us to be able to invest enough time to nurture our relationships.

"Make it your ambition to lead a quiet life, to mind your own business and to work with your hands, just as we told you, so that your daily life may win the respect of outsiders and so that you will not be dependent on anybody" (1 Thessalonians 4:11-12).

6. Success is meaningless apart from serving Jesus Christ

King Solomon had an annual income of more than £50 million (our estimate). He lived in a palace that took 13 years to build. He owned 40,000 stalls of horses. The daily menu of his household included 100 sheep and 30 oxen. Obviously, Solomon was in a position to know whether money would bring true fulfillment. He concluded, *"Utterly meaningless! Everything is meaningless"* (Ecclesiastes 1:2).

7. Do not be conformed to this world

Romans 12:2 tells us, *"Do not conform any longer to the pattern of this world."* We are constantly bombarded with advertising to prompt us to spend money. No matter what the product - clothing, deodorants, credit cards, or anything else - the message is clear: the happy, beautiful, wrinkle-free life can be ours if we are willing to buy it. The reality is that many buy things they do not need, with money they do not have, to impress people they do not even like."

Poverty, prosperity or stewardship?

1. Violating scriptural principles

Joshua 1:8 says: *"This Book of the Law shall not depart from your mouth, but you shall meditate in it day and night, that you may observe to do according to all that is written in it. For then you will make your way prosperous, and then you will have good success"* (NKJV). There is a requirement to do all that is written in the Bible. A person may be giving generously but acting dishonestly. A person may be honest but not fulfilling work responsibilities. A person may be a faithful employee but up to his ears in debt. A person may be completely out of debt but not giving. Those who do not understand all the requirements often neglect areas of responsibility unknowingly and suffer financially.

2. Building godly character

In Romans 5:3-4 we read, *"suffering produces perseverance; perseverance, character; and character, hope."* Many godly people in the Bible lived righteously, yet they lost their possessions. David became a national hero after slaying Goliath, only to be forced to flee for his life from a tormented King Saul. Job lost his children and possessions in the space of a few moments and was described as a *"blameless and upright, a man who fears God and shuns evil"* (Job 1:8).

God moulds our character by allowing us to experience difficult circumstances. Our heavenly Father knows us better than we know ourselves. In His infinite wisdom He knows exactly how much He can entrust to us at any time without harming us.

3. Our dependence and His discipline

Hebrews 12:6, 10 tells us that, *"The Lord disciplines those he loves for our good…so that we may share in his holiness."*

If we have sin in our lives or a wrong attitude toward money, out of the Lord's great love for us he may discipline us by allowing financial difficulties to encourage us to forsake our sin.

4. The mystery of God's sovereignty

In Hebrews 11 we find "Faith's Hall of Fame." In verses 1-35 we have a list of people who triumphed miraculously by exercising their faith in God. But in verse 36 the writer directs our attention to godly people who gained God's approval, yet experienced poverty. God ultimately chooses how much to entrust to each person, and sometimes we simply can't understand His decisions.

Module seven
Honesty

All of us have to make daily decisions about whether or not to handle money honestly. Do we tell the other person when we receive too much change? Have you ever tried to sell something and been tempted not to tell the whole truth because you might lose the sale?

These decisions are made more difficult because many people around us seem to be acting dishonestly. God, however, wants us to be completely honest. There are hundreds of verses in the Bible that communicate the Lord's desire for us to be totally honest. *"The Lord detests lying lips..."* (Proverbs 12:22). *"The Lord hates...a lying tongue..."* (Proverbs 6:16-17). *"Do not steal. Do not lie. Do not deceive one another"* (Leviticus 19:11). *"Each of you must put off falsehood and speak truthfully to his neighbour, for we are all members of one body.... He who has been stealing must steal no longer, but must work, doing something useful with his own hands, that he may have something to share with those in need"* (Ephesians 4:25, 28).

1. Truthfulness is one of God's attributes

The Lord is identified as the truth. *"I am...the truth"* (John 14:6). And the Lord commands us to reflect His honest and holy character: *"...Be holy in all you do; for it is written, 'Be holy, because I am holy'"* (1 Peter 1:15-16). God's nature is in contrast to Satan's. John 8:44 describes the devil's character: *".... He* [the devil] *was a murderer from the beginning, not holding to the truth, for there is no truth in him. When he lies, he speaks his native language, for he is a liar and the father of lies."* The Lord wants us to conform to His honest character rather than to the dishonest nature of the devil.

2. Why God has established the standard of honesty

A. We cannot be dishonest and love God
"He whose walk is upright fears the Lord, but he whose ways are devious despises him" (Proverbs 14:2). When we are dishonest, we act as if the living God does not even exist! We believe that God is able to provide exactly what we need, for He has promised to do so: *...seek first his kingdom and his righteousness, and all these things will be given to you as well* (Matthew 6:33). We also act as if God is incapable of discovering our dishonesty and is powerless to discipline us. If we

really believe God will discipline us, then we will not consider acting dishonestly. Honest behaviour is an issue of faith. An honest decision may look foolish in light of what we can see, but the godly person knows Jesus Christ is alive, even though invisible. Every honest decision we make strengthens our faith in God.

B. We cannot be dishonest and love our neighbour

"The commandments, 'Do not steal,' 'Do not covet,' and whatever other commandment there may be, are summed up in this one rule: 'Love your neighbour as yourself.' Love does no harm to its neighbour..." (Romans 13:9-10). When we act dishonestly, we are stealing from another person. Even though we might justify dishonesty by believing it is against a business or the Government, ultimately, the victims are always people. The business owners or the taxpayers are the ones suffering loss.

C. Honesty establishes credibility

So that evangelism can be effective. Honest behaviour enables us to demonstrate the reality of Jesus Christ to those who do not yet know Him. It confirms that we serve a holy God. *"So that you may become blameless and pure, children of God without fault in a crooked and depraved generation, in which you shine like stars in the universe"* (Philippians 2:15).

D. Honesty confirms God's direction

Proverbs 4:24-26 reads, *"Put away from you a deceitful mouth and put devious lips far from you. Let your eyes look directly ahead and let your gaze be fixed straight in front of you. Watch the path of your feet and all your ways will be established"* (NASB). As you are honest...all your ways will be established. Choosing to walk the narrow path of honesty eliminates the many possible avenues of dishonesty.

E. It is important to be honest in small things

The smallest acts of dishonesty lead to greater dishonesty. *"...Whoever is dishonest with very little will also be dishonest with much"* (Luke 16:10).

3. Escaping the temptation to be dishonest

A. Submit to the Holy Spirit

If we do not live our lives yielded to the Holy Spirit, all of us will be dishonest. *"...Live by the Spirit, and you will not gratify the desires of the sinful nature. For the sinful nature desires what is contrary to the Spirit, and the Spirit what is contrary to the sinful nature..."* (Galatians 5:16-17). The desire of our human nature is to act dishonestly. *"...Out of men's hearts come evil thoughts...theft...deceit...."* (Mark 7:21-

22). The desire of the Spirit is for us to be completely honest. The totally honest life is supernatural. We must submit ourselves entirely to Jesus Christ as Lord and allow Him to live His life through us. There is no other way.

B. Have a healthy fear of discipline

God is a loving Father who disciplines His children for their benefit. *"No discipline seems pleasant at the time, but painful. Later on, however, it produces a harvest of righteousness and peace for those who have been trained by it"* (Hebrews 12:11). One of the ways God uses to motivate us to honest living is by having a "healthy fear." Proverbs 16:6 reads, *"...Through the fear of the Lord a man avoids evil."* If you are a parent and one of your children steals something, do you allow the child to keep it? No, you insist it is returned because the child's character would be harmed if he or she kept stolen property. And you want the child to experience enough discomfort to produce a lasting impression. When our heavenly Father lovingly disciplines us, it is usually done in such a way that we will not forget.

C. Surround yourself with honest people

Scripture teaches that we are influenced by those around us, either for good or evil. *"Do not be misled: 'Bad company corrupts good character'"* (1 Corinthians 15:33). *"The accomplice of a thief is his own enemy..."* (Proverbs 29:24). We are not to isolate ourselves from everyone who is dishonest; in fact, we are to be salt and light in the world. However, it is much easier to remain honest if you are surrounded by other honest people

4. What to do when dishonest

A. Restore fellowship with God

Anytime we are dishonest, we sin and break our fellowship with our Lord. This needs to be restored. First John 1:9 tells us how: *"If we confess our sins, He is faithful and just and will forgive us our sins and purify us from all unrighteousness."* We must agree with God that our dishonesty was sin, and then thankfully accept God's gracious forgiveness so we can again enjoy His fellowship.

B. Return everything received dishonestly to its rightful owner

If we have acquired anything dishonestly, we must return it to its rightful owner. This is called restitution. *"When he thus sins and becomes guilty, he must return what he has stolen or taken by extortion, or what was entrusted to him, or lost property he found"* (Leviticus 6:4). Restitution is an effort to correct a wrong. Zacchaeus is a good example of fulfilling this principle. He promised Jesus, *"...If I have cheated anybody out of anything, I will pay back four times the amount"* (Luke 19:8).

5. Blessings and curses

The Lord has promised blessings for the honest, while curses are reserved for the dishonest.

Blessings for the honest:

- Blessing of a more intimate relationship with the Lord. *"For the devious are an abomination to the Lord; but He is intimate with the upright"* (Proverbs 3:32, NASB).

- Blessings on the family. *"The righteous man leads a blameless life; blessed are his children after him"* (Proverbs 20:7).

- Blessings of life. *"Truthful lips endure forever, but a lying tongue lasts only a moment"* (Proverbs 12:19).

- Blessings of prosperity. *"The house of the righteous contains great treasure, but the income of the wicked brings them trouble"* (Proverbs 15:6).

Curses reserved for the dishonest:

- Curse of alienation from God. *"For the devious are an abomination to the Lord…"* (Proverbs 3:32, NASB).

- Curse on the family. *"A greedy man brings trouble to his family…"* (Proverbs 15:27).

- Curse of death. *"A fortune made by a lying tongue is a fleeting vapour and a deadly snare"* (Proverbs 21:6).

- Curse of poverty. *"Dishonest money dwindles away…"* (Proverbs 13:11).

6. Bribes

A bribe is anything given to a person to influence him to act in the giver's favour. The taking of bribes is prohibited in Scripture. *"Do not accept a bribe, for a bribe blinds those who see and twists the words of the righteous"* (Exodus 23:8). *"A wicked man accepts a bribe in secret to pervert the course of justice"* (Proverbs 17:23). Bribes can come in the form of money, gifts, and promotions. God will not bless anyone who is dishonest and gives or receives a bribe.

- *"The Lord hates cheating and delights in honesty"* (Proverbs 11:1, TLB).

- *"The upright are directed by their honesty; the wicked fall beneath their load of sin"* (Proverbs 11:5, TLB).

- *"The good influence of godly citizens causes a city to prosper, but the moral decay of the wicked drives it downhill"* (Proverbs 11:11, NLT).

- The Lord hates the stubborn but delights in those who are good" (Proverbs 11:20, NLT).

Module eight
Giving

Giving is one of the most fulfilling parts of the Christian life. Throughout the Bible we are encouraged to be generous. In fact, there are more verses related to giving than any other subject dealing with money.

1. It is important to give with the proper attitude

A. Give out of a heart of love

It is hard to imagine anything more worthy of praise than giving everything to the poor. But if it is done with the wrong attitude, without love, it is no benefit to the giver. *"If I give all I possess to the poor...but have not love, I gain nothing"* (1 Corinthians 13:3). God evaluates our giving based on our attitude. Jesus said in Matthew 23:23: *"Woe to you, teachers of the law and Pharisees, you hypocrites! You give a tenth of your spices - mint, dill and cummin. But you have neglected the more important matters of the law - justice, mercy and faithfulness. You should have practiced the latter, without neglecting the former."* The Pharisees had been careful to give the correct amount - down to the last mint leaf in their gardens. However, for giving to be of any value to the giver, it must be done out of love. God the Father set the example of giving in love. *"For God so loved the world that he gave his one and only Son"* (John 3:16). The best way to give in love is to give each gift as if you are giving it directly to Jesus Christ. When you give to the Lord, it can be an act of worship because God is our Saviour and our faithful provider.

B. Give cheerfully

"Each man should give what he has decided in his heart to give, not reluctantly or under compulsion, for God loves a cheerful giver" (2 Corinthians 9:7). The word translated "reluctantly" means with sorrow, grief or annoyance. The word translated "cheerful" means joyful, happy, and exuberant. We are not to give reluctantly; rather we should give because we are joyful about the opportunity

to help others. Stop and examine yourself. What is your attitude toward giving? It is very important to give with the proper attitude.

2. Give to God first

Part of our responsibility as a faithful steward is to give back to God a portion of what He has entrusted to us. *"Honour the Lord from your wealth, with the firstfruits of all your crops"* (Proverbs 3:9). God doesn't need our money, but we need to give. Giving to the Lord is a reminder that God owns all we possess and that He is our Provider. It is also an indicator of our obedience to God's principles.

3. The amount to give

I am convinced that a tithe, or ten per cent of our income, is the foundation of our giving, *"...Yet you rob me...in tithes and offerings. You are under a curse - the whole nation of you - because you are robbing me"* (Malachi 3:8-9). In addition to the tithe, God's people in the Old Testament gave offerings. The New Testament builds on the foundation of tithes and offerings, teaching us to give in proportion to what we receive. Jesus praised sacrificial giving. *"A poor widow came and put in two very small copper coins, worth only a fraction of a penny.... Jesus said, 'I tell you the truth, this poor widow has put more into the treasury than all the others. They all gave out of their wealth; but she, out of her poverty, put in everything - all she had to live on'"* (Mark 12:42-44).

4. The blessings of giving

"...Remembering the words the Lord Jesus himself said: 'It is more blessed to give than to receive'" (Acts 20:35). If a gift is given with a proper attitude, the giver benefits in four ways.

A. Giving draws our hearts toward Christ
Above all else, giving directs our heart to Christ. *"For where your treasure is, there your heart will be also"* (Matthew 6:21). This is why it is necessary to give each gift to Jesus Christ. When you give your gift to Him, your heart will automatically be drawn to the Lord.

B. Giving develops godly character and helps us conform to Christ
Our heavenly Father wants His children to be conformed to the image of Jesus Christ whose character is that of an unselfish giver. Unfortunately, humans are

naturally selfish. One of the ways we become conformed to Christ is by giving.

C. Giving allows us to put treasures in heaven

Matthew 6:20 reads, *"But store up for yourselves treasures in heaven, where moth and rust do not destroy, and where thieves do not break in and steal"* (Matthew 6:20). The Lord wants us to know that we can invest for eternity. Paul wrote, *"Not that I am looking for a gift, but I am looking for what may be credited to your account"* (Philippians 4:17). When we give I believe there is an "account" for each of us in heaven, an account we will enjoy for eternity.

D. Giving can produce a material increase to the giver

"One man gives freely, yet gains even more; another withholds unduly, but comes to poverty. A generous man will prosper; he who refreshes others will himself be refreshed" (Proverbs 11:24-25).

"...Whoever sows sparingly will also reap sparingly, and whoever sows generously will also reap generously.... God is able to make all grace abound to you, so that in all things at all times, having all that you need, you will abound in every good work. As it is written: 'He has scattered abroad his gifts to the poor; his righteousness endures forever.' Now he who supplies seed to the sower and bread for food will also supply and increase your store of seed and will enlarge the harvest of your righteousness. You will be made rich in every way so that you can be generous on every occasion..." (2 Corinthians 9:6, 8-11).

These verses teach that giving results in a material increase: *"will also reap generously…in all things at all times…having all that you need…you will abound… will supply and increase your store of seed…enlarge the harvest…you will be made rich in every way."* But note why the Lord is returning an increase: *"so that you can be generous on every occasion."* The Lord provides a material increase so that we may give more and have our needs met at the same time.

5. To whom should we give?

Scripture encourages us to give to the work of Christ and to the needy.

A. Give to the local Church, Christian workers and ministries

The Bible tells us to give to the Church and those serving in ministry. Old Testament priests were to receive support: *"I give to the Levites all the tithes in Israel...in return for the work they do..."* (Numbers 18:21). And the New Testament teaching on support is just as strong. *"Elders who do their work well should be respected and paid well, especially those who work hard at both preaching and teaching"*

(1 Timothy 5:17, TLB). *"...The Lord has commanded that those who preach the gospel should receive their living from the gospel"* (1 Corinthians 9:14).

In our opinion, a minimum of ten per cent of our income should be given to our Church. But we also believe we should give to others who are teaching us. *"Anyone who receives instruction in the word must share all good things with his instructor"* (Galatians 6:6).

B. Give to the poor

Hundreds of verses deal with meeting the needs of the poor. In Matthew 25:34-45 we learn one of the most exciting truths in Scripture. *"The King will say...'I was hungry and you gave me something to eat, I was thirsty and you gave me something to drink.'...Then the righteous will answer him, 'Lord, when did we see you hungry, and feed you, or thirsty and give you something to drink?'....The King will reply, 'I tell you the truth, whatever you did for one of the least of these brothers of mine, you did for me.' Then he will say to those on his left, 'Depart from me, you who are cursed, into the eternal fire.... I was hungry and you gave me nothing to eat, I was thirsty and you gave me nothing to drink.... Whatever you did not do for one of the least of these, you did not do for me.'"*

Jesus, the Saviour of the world, identifies Himself with the poor. When we give to the poor, we are actually giving to Jesus. *"Whoever is kind to the needy honours God"* (Proverbs 14:31). *"A generous man will himself be blessed, for he shares his food with the poor"* (Proverbs 22:9). *"All they* [the apostles] *asked was that we should continue to remember the poor, the very thing I* [Paul] *was eager to do"* (Galatians 2:10).

Module nine
Investing

Scripture encourages saving

"The wise man saves for the future, but the foolish man spends whatever he gets" (Proverbs 21:20 TLB).

We are encouraged to save to prepare for future needs. Saving means not spending today so you will have something to spend in the future. Joseph is an example of a person who saved. In Genesis 41, Joseph saved during the seven years of plenty so that there would be enough to live on during the seven years of famine.

A. Save only if also giving

Jesus told this parable, *"...The ground of a certain rich man produced a good crop. He thought to himself, 'What shall I do? I have no place to store my crops.' Then he said, 'This is what I'll do. I will tear down my barns and build bigger ones, and there I will store all my grain and my goods. And I'll say to myself, "You have plenty of good things laid up for many years. Take life easy; eat, drink and be merry."' But God said to him, 'You fool! This very night your life will be demanded from you...' This is how it will be for anyone who stores up things for himself but is not rich toward God.... For where your treasure is, there your heart will be also"* (Luke 12:16-21, 34). God called the rich man a fool because he saved all of his goods and was not giving generously. The only time we should be saving is when we are giving so that our hearts will remain focused on the Lord.

B. Save regularly

"Steady plodding brings prosperity; hasty speculation brings poverty" (Proverbs 21:5 TLB). The fundamental principle you need to practice to become a successful saver is to spend less than you earn. Then save and invest the difference over a long period of time. You do not have to earn a lot of money; rather, save consistently. *"Go to the ant, you sluggard; consider its ways and be wise! It has no commander, no overseer or ruler, yet it stores its provisions in summer and gathers its food at harvest"* (Proverbs 6:6-8).

C. How much should we save?

There is only one biblical example of saving that specifies an amount. Joseph saved twenty per cent per year during seven years of plenty so that the nation would have enough food for the following seven years of famine. *"Let Pharaoh appoint commissioners over the land to take a fifth of the harvest of Egypt during the seven years of abundance"* (Genesis 41:34). In our opinion, it is wise to attempt to save ten per cent of our income.

What to save for:

1. Save for unexpected emergencies
In our opinion, it is wise to save for unexpected expenses so we can use cash rather than incur debt. If possible, start by saving one week's income and build this up to two months so that you can cover at least two months of regular expenses.

2. Save for major purchases
Save for major purchases such as a house, car or education.

3. Save for longer-term needs
Once you have saved for unexpected emergencies and major purchases, it is wise to save for longer-term needs, such as providing for old age.

Investments

People place some of their savings in investments with the expectation of receiving an income or growth in value. Investments vary according to the individual's attitude toward investment. Some save in collective investments (e.g. unit trusts) others in savings accounts or directly on the stock market.

1. Avoid risky investments
"There is another serious problem I have seen everywhere – savings are put into risky investments that turn sour, and soon there is nothing left to pass on to one's son. The man who speculates is soon back to where he began - with nothing. This, as I said, is a very serious problem, for all his hard work has been for nothing; he has been working for the wind. It is all swept away" (Ecclesiastes 5:13-16 TLB).

2. Diversify investments
It is usually wise not to put all our money into one investment. *"Divide your portion to seven, or even to eight, for you do not know what misfortune may occur on the earth"* (Ecclesiastes 11:2, NASB). There is no investment without risk, and Scripture does not recommend any specific investments.

Gambling

The Bible does not specifically prohibit gambling or gaming; however, many who gamble do so to get rich quickly. This is a violation of Scripture. *"A man with an evil eye hastens after wealth and does not know that want will come upon him"* (Proverbs 28:22, NASB). Make a commitment never to gamble, even for entertainment. We should not expose ourselves to the risk of becoming compulsive gamblers, nor should we support an industry that enslaves so many.

Module ten
Eternity

1. Life on earth is brief

"...What is your life? You are a mist that appears for a little while and then vanishes" (James 4:14).

2. Number your days on earth

"The length of our days is seventy years-or eighty, if we have the strength.... Teach us to number our days aright, that we may gain a heart of wisdom" (Psalm 90:10, 12). Value each day you have left on earth, keeping in mind that none of us has a certainty of even one more day.

3. God will judge everyone according to his or her deeds

"...For we will all stand before God's judgment seat.... So then, each of us will give an account of himself to God" (Romans 14:10-12).

    A. All believers in Christ, although spending eternity with the Lord in heaven, will gain or lose eternal rewards. *"...Work will be shown for what it is; because the Day will bring it to light...the fire will test the quality of each man's work. If what he has built survives, he will receive his reward. If it is burned up, he will suffer loss..."* (1 Corinthians 3:13-15).

    B. Our works are what we have done with our time, skills, money and possessions during our life on earth. Today's sacrifices and service for Christ will result in rewards you will enjoy forever.

4. Our daily choices determine what happens in the future

"...Man is destined to die once, and after that to face judgement" (Hebrews 9:27). We only live on this earth once. There is no such thing as reincarnation. What we do in this life is of eternal importance. When we are face-to-face with Christ and look back on our life, we'll want to see that the things in which we invested our time and money are big things to the Lord.

An Overview of the Practical Application Workbook

While the small group *Student Manual* looks at a spiritual understanding of what the Bible has to say about how we handle our money and possessions as an individual and shared group resource; the *Practical Application Workbook* is a personal workbook only.

During the ten-week study students are asked to carry out a series of financial exercises that will enable them to take control of their finances and apply the spiritual lessons they acquire from the *Student Manual*.

Over ten weeks the *Practical Application Workbook* leads the student on a journey that enables them to look at and plan:

- Preparing a balanced spending plan

- Their record keeping and balancing the books

- Filing records

- Preparing a personal financial statement

- Completing an ownership deed

- Debt repayment plan

- Estate planning

- Will preparation

- Insurance protection

- Saving and investing

- Life goals

1. The form centre – please refer to page 89

We are aware that a system with 17 forms may seem a little unwieldy. However you will see that the forms cover four key planning areas:

A. Primary forms (FC1-5)
These are the forms that are at the heart of helping students prepare and manage their balanced spending plan.

B. Secondary forms (FC6-10)

The first two (FC6 and FC7) are only used for the first four weeks while FC8-10 are individual records to record cash, bank and card spending.

C. Debt forms (FC11-FC13)

These three forms are to help those in debt develop a strategy to repay their debt.

D. Financial planning forms (FC14-FC17)

These four forms enable students to take a look at their current finances and organise their thoughts with regard to estate and insurance planning.

How many forms need to be completed on an ongoing basis?

One - the spending budget, but we strongly recommend that writing up the cash, bank and card records will help most students work out what to record on their spending budget.

2. Are these available online?

The spreadsheets are available in Excel on My Crown. The read-only file can either be used with the fields fixed as they are in the workbook or, alternatively, the password crown007 can be used to open up the file and for this to be adapted as each student wishes. As ever, when opening the file formats may be lost.

The My Crown area also contains a PDF file of all forms. It may help to have copies of these forms.

3. First six weeks

Over the first four weeks students record their expenditure before preparing their budgets in weeks 5 and 6.

4. Weeks 7 to 10

In week 7 students start implementing their plans while in weeks 8-10 they look at other areas of planning, including insurance and estate planning.

There are comprehensive notes on the work to be completed each week in the workbook. In some of the weeks (2, 4 and 9) the practical work aligns with the subject matter of the *Student Manual*.

5. Matt and Jennifer samples

Wherever possible we have included samples of the completed forms as a guide to completion.

And now, a look at each module in more depth:

Module one
Getting started

At your launch meeting when you hand out the Crown study books please encourage students to complete the first seven days of the spending tracker (FC 6) immediately prior to their first Crown group meeting.

Make sure all students have registered on My Crown (www.crownuk.org) as this will enable them to access our other online resources. Each week they should also read the background notes in the practical module. The first week requires students to start completing their first month's spending tracker in which they record all income and expenditure whether through their bank, cash or card accounts. It is important that expenditure from all methods is recorded as the overall pattern of expenditure may change during the course of the month.

Filing. Most people have a way of filing their receipts, but encourage everyone to look at their filing – there is a recommended suggestion in module one.

Module two
Financial position

Continue with the first month's spending tracker.

Personal financial statement (FC14)
While this looks a little like a daunting accountancy exercise it is intended to provide a helpful approach for students to identify their assets and liabilities – what they own and what they owe. Encourage everyone to complete this, even if the numbers are approximate (maybe to the nearest thousand). This is not just a numbers exercise, it is also an important aspect of the module two study in which we learn that everything belongs to God.

Why split the assets between short term and long term?
Students may have assets but may be experiencing cash flow difficulties. As is shown in the example of Matt and Jennifer, Matt has net assets of £72,500, but

current liabilities of £3,500. If Matt doesn't have a balanced budget he may find it difficult to repay his debts which may hamper his ability to pay his bills as and when they are due.

Deed of ownership (page 15)

This deed is not a binding legal document! However, it is an important step for students to take to acknowledge that everything belongs to God. The form provides the opportunity for you to have this witnessed by another group member. If you do not feel comfortable with this or if you wish to come back to this at a later time, that's your decision – you are the Crown leader.

Module three
Spending

Continue with the first month's spending tracker.

By now everyone will be used to filling in the first month's spending tracker. Experience shows that some people will be surprised where their money is going and perhaps even be thinking of changing their spending habits. Our practical work this week focuses on seeing how many of the 17 general spending strategies might be applicable while there are four pages of specific spending tips - in fact there are more than 60 tips this week. Some will not apply, but some may.

Idea list (FC7)

Reviewing these suggestions may result in ideas for reducing expenditure, raising cash by selling assets or increasing income. Capture these on the idea list.

Module four
Debt (FC11-FC13)

This week sees the completion of the first month's spending tracker.

This is one of the weeks where the spiritual work is aligned to the practical. Many people who attend the Crown course are in debt and these two modules together provide a robust opportunity to address how to reduce debts. The debt snowball strategy is proven to reduce debt £ for £ faster than any other approach. It also provides an incentive by seeing the number of debts reduce with the emphasis on focusing all possible resources on repaying the smallest debt. The 'My Crown' area has a debt snowball calculator which enables you to enter debt data and see this calculate the interest saved using the debt snowball approach.

Module five
Budgeting one: The spending budget (FC1)

With the spending tracker completed we are now ready to start work on preparing the spending budget. Modules five and six are probably the toughest of all the ten weeks so make sure you take time to review what steps are needed to complete the budget. In order to prepare a budget for any particular line item there are a number of steps to be taken. These are explained in the workbook. The spending tracker contains some valuable information, but it may not indicate a true average monthly cost. For example, it is possible that while recording expenditure the student decided to change their spending habits. It is possible that some expenditure did not arise in that month. For example no council tax is normally payable in February or March. Therefore the actual expenditure that is transferred from the spending tracker to the spending budget (FC1) is useful information, but not to be regarded in isolation without applying the five spending tests. Follow these steps and you are well on your way to producing the first draft of a spending budget.

Periodic expenses (FC 3)
In step 3 (Page 35) certain non-recurring expenditure is identified and excluded from the detailed budget on FC1 – we call these periodic expenses because they do not occur on a regular monthly basis. These expenses should now be included on FC3 when applying the principles in the five spending tests, totalled and then divided by 12 to establish an average monthly cost. This monthly budget should then be entered on the spending budget and a separate bank account set up especially to receive the monthly transfer and pay the budgeted periodic expenses.

Key point: The setting up of a separate 'periodic account' is the key to ensuring there are adequate funds when those non-recurring costs arise.

Module six
Budgeting two: The spending plan (FC2)
This week we transfer the month's spending budget (FC 3) to the spending plan (FC2) and then, as with the first month's spending tracker, this form is for recording all expenditure. At the end of the month the expenditure should be totalled and the surplus/deficit for each of the items of income or expenditure written down. Note that the only entry in the periodic column is the monthly

transfer. Any payments that are budgeted as periodic expenses should be paid out of the periodic (bank) account.

The remainder of this module has the forms for recording bank transactions (not forgetting direct debits and cash withdrawals), cash (including cash from the hole in the wall, supermarket cashback etc.) and credit or store card transactions.

The purpose of these forms is three-fold:

1. Keeping an eye on the balance (cards only) that is accumulating and must be repaid
2. Developing an approach to accounting for cash which can so easily 'disappear'
3. Having a separate record of payments that need to be transferred to the spending plan

The final part of this week's work is to look at the mechanics of balancing the bank account. How many people look at the balance in the electronic machine without reconciling it to see what outstanding payments have not yet been processed by the bank? Seems like this is what accountants do, but nevertheless it is surprising how many people are caught out by looking at their own bank records as opposed to what the bank balance reads.

Module seven
Implementation

While it is going to be another few weeks before the first month's plan is complete, we will look ahead to the end of the month to see what steps have to be taken to review and balance the finances. We recommend that as leader you read the notes and go through the examples to show how this works.

Periodic expenses tracker (FC4)
The individual payments each month should be recorded in the respective month's column. It is important to keep an eye on the expenditure and see that this is roughly in line with budget. If it appears that the budget is inadequate (e.g. energy costs increasing) then it will be necessary to increase the periodic expense transfer.

Month end tracker summary (FC5)
The spending plan notes show how to calculate the month's surplus or deficit. The month end tracker (FC 5) provides the information to assess what action may be necessary to keep the finances on target. Maybe household finances

need to be tightened next month? Maybe a transfer needs to be made from savings? Maybe debt has been incurred and a short term plan made for repayment.

Module eight
Estate planning

With the hard work complete, at least we hope that is the case, we now start to look at some other aspects of financial planning. The introductory notes highlight the danger of not having a Will and the *Practical Application Workbook* stresses the importance of having a Will. Does the Church leadership have a legal adviser they can recommend, or ideally two so as to provide choice?

Organising your estate (FC15)
This form provides opportunity to agree some key points for inclusion in the Will. We all know we're going to die (but we think, probably not just yet, so this can wait a while!). Remember we don't know when we will depart to eternity and it makes a lot of sense to tie up as many loose ends as possible.

Module nine
Investing

Written by two Christian IFAs, this module looks at saving and investing and the role of insurance.

Saving and investing
We recommend that everyone has some savings that can be accessed to deal with emergencies, e.g. breakdown of household equipment. Maybe initially building up one week's earnings, then one month and then maybe two months might provide cover so that household finances do not suffer irretrievable breakdown in the event of an unexpected expense. We need to have ready savings because we never know when something unexpected could happen.

Organising your insurance (FC16)
There are a range of views regarding insurance. Some say, 'never' and others 'absolutely.' The worksheet asks questions and allows students to consider what happens if one of the partners to a marriage dies. He or she may be the main breadwinner. Is there any desire to have the mortgage paid off (if mortgage protection does not exist)? Is it appropriate to provide a capital sum

or an ongoing income? This worksheet stops a long way from the point where advice is given. It is right and proper that professional advice be sought by any student wishing to look at their own situation. Again, does the Church leadership wish to recommend a professional?

Experience from Crown studies indicates that students appreciate the opportunity to consider these areas.

Module ten
Life goals (FC17)

While the *Student Manual* focuses on eternity our practical study looks at life goals. Some people love looking at their goals, others run a mile. Maybe some who have no goals will think about what they might achieve. While there is rightly a slant toward financial goals it maybe that some take the opportunity to consider their goals generally. How could they [better] serve God? What do they wish to do differently? What do they wish to achieve?

And finally
I would like to thank you for your commitment to bringing Crown biblical studies to your Church. Everyone at Crown wishes you success with using the Crown studies.

If we can be of further service, do please contact us. All our contact details can be found on www.crownuk.org.

Crown Small Group Study-Live

On the DVD you have a sample of how to run a Crown small group study.

At the conclusion of this DVD training event, Rhoda gathered together a number of students from our own Church Crown groups. Join them and gain an insight into how we facilitate our groups.